# Escape from Wreck City

# Acknowledgements

Thank you to the editors and staff of the following journals where poems from this book first appeared: *The Antigonish Review, Arc, The Best Canadian Poetry in English 2011, CV2, Event, Fiddlehead, Grain, Kootenay Mountain Culture, subTerrain,* and *Vallum.*

Many thanks and much gratitude to Brian Kaufman at Anvil Press for his interest and support. Thanks also to Tom Wayman for his early encouragement and continued support. I'd also like to thank my close friend Luke Maclean who has been whistling praise for as long as I can remember. Lastly, thanks to my wife Darragh and all friends and family.

# Escape from Wreck City

*poems by*

**John Creary**

anvil press / vancouver

Anvil Press Publishers Inc.
P.O. Box 3008, Main Post Office
Vancouver, B.C. V6B 3X5  Canada
www.anvilpress.com


Library and Archives Canada Cataloguing in Publication

Creary, John, author
        Escape from Wreck City / John Creary.

Poems.

ISBN 978-1-77214-096-5 (paperback)

[Full CIP entry available upon request.]


Printed and bound in Canada
Cover illustration by John Creary
Interior by HeimatHouse
Represented in Canada by Publishers Group Canada
Distributed by Raincoast Books

The publisher gratefully acknowledges the financial assistance of the Canada Council for the Arts, the Canada Book Fund, and the Province of British Columbia through the B.C. Arts Council and the Book Publishing Tax Credit.

PRINTED AND BOUND IN CANADA

*For Nolan*

# CONTENTS

## III

## IV

I

# The Great Northern Poem

has not been written. No, but it is here. It's there, North of your first breath, North of your free speech. North of going bald or being blind. North of crumpled papers filling the wicker basket like a small castle. North of all that. North of a dark mountain cave and North of a dead house pet. North of conversations with strangers in the wind or at the bus stop. It's North of Billy Collins and North of Kenneth Rexroth. It's North of winning at Scrabble with the word icy or igloo. It's up North of five dollars and five million for that matter. It's North of Ikea, North of daydreams of climbing tall limber trees and certainly North of motherly advice. I can see it, North of your smoking father and North, yes, of your cousin Ted. It's North of New York and a new San Francisco. It's North of the road and North of the road less traveled. It's Northbound on an old train trudging towards a blazing horizon. It's North of yesterday and a brand new millennium. It's North of no parking and North of the entire kafuffle. It's North of sitting on the fence. North of superheroes with bad breath and getting even with cold enemies. Yes, it *is* slightly North of a genuine smile. North of the plague, the dentist, and unfortunately, the florist. It's North of Stockholm syndrome and a WestJet seat sale. It can be seen over there, moving North in the headlights of a speeding sports car. It's so far North of the American Dream and you would be surprised how far North it is of dying young. It's North of smoking pot and seeing God in North Korea. It's North of Iraq and North of trying to forget an atrocity. It's North of middle ground and North of losing some too. It's North of drowning in an almost empty bathtub. It's North of a drunken tangent and North of making the magic last. I assure you, it's North of where you sit and North of this moment. But just North of this poem, stumbling through a blizzard, this is what I meant to show you.

# Escape from Wreck City

The things you mumbled
at your tattooist's

cold apartment
had little consequence.

You said the honour
of public greatness

is to be sweetly veiled
in pigeon droppings.

Having recently discovered
sherry you've forgotten

most of the last month.
Still, I'm enchanted

with how you let
the word Dubrovnik

roll around your mouth
like some forgotten

tonic. You sprawled out
in the witchgrass

like a wounded insomniac
and this prism you insist

I window wash
has a crooked bullseye

slumped around a gross
misunderstanding

of what it really means
to act like evil twins.

There is only one true
vandal; let your eyes

orbit around the room.
You're mumbling again;

it sounds like you're saying
I'm fond of widows.

We're moving inappropriately
through Amontillado,

lightly headed for a mile
wide in-limbo.

Do you ever want to poke
around in the sticky

ink of something more
intimate? Less rhetorical?

I'm an old car in mint
condition. You're marooned

in an equinox as the melon
queen of tattoo parlors.

# IMO

1.
The fake surfers are tired, cool jumping
All the time, waiting for the big nowhere.

2.
Life has become a series of interludes,
Inspired moments between the puddles.

3.
Basic seduction starts with light
Kissing around the neck, post-cocktail massage.

4.
The devolution to sound bytes and blurbs in life
was predictable; first language, then whole existence.

5.
Political parties should be wry, pluck party names
Like bands — Hospital Bombers or Thieves like Us.

6.
The fake surfers are mad, they can't spell
Audacious or even debut. They are cursed, obviously.

7.
The final act could be called the great miasma and
In my opinion, the fumes are beautiful.

# Short Fuse

I snort cocaine off my electric guitar, spin
and pu-puncture a raw set with heat.

My body combats a swelling cluster of hip-
sters in scarves and tight jeans. Two billion

basement eyes jumping near the silhouette
of my moment. Buzzed, unshaven, shackled

in the hell of a rock star, slamming shots
of Jager, drowning bad news with designer

drugs. I am a short fuse, a maniac and a failed
lover, flailing my skeleton, wasted in this dream.

I dance, dance, dance neurotic, circle backstage,
blackout on amphetamines, kicking the intestine

of a squawking police car, kissing the gutter
mouth on your cities East Side. My new band

is a stage grenade — somebody look at me.
My chest hair spills out and off the playlist,

chasing the heart shaped wrench of my teenage
fan club. Take a chance, girl. I'm writing a blog,

posing on warped and wobbling tabletops. Hey,
Reggie! Turn the volume up and take my picture.

# Woman, Camera

Her flesh is a secret, a hushed storyboard,
a soft canvas for the lightning of cameras.

Her voice, shy and unfamiliar, giggles
self-consciously, complements her green eyes.

Her gaze is enormous, a museum in HD,
a sort of seductive lava melting the frames.

She is graceful in black and white, blatant,
stretching her limbs electric across the bed.

We can feel her pulse in the composition,
her heartbeat when she peeks at the dreamcity

through a cracked window, begging the angels
of the small world to sing her a meandering love song.

# The Adventures of Cloud Nothing and Pill Wonder

This year lacks the bit-lip tension
of last year, at least

that's what's been steaming around
the lit pipes of the rumour mill.

Summertime; Cloud Nothing and Pill Wonder
pretend each tomorrow

is a birthday, complete with familiar
grin, a work-in-progress,

half nelson's and hangovers. Let's watch
the sunset, Pill Wonder

said to no one in particular and wandered
off towards the rotting grey bridge.

I remember being just kids, barely
skinny teens, stealing

a glimpse at girls in open windows,
praying for the marvel, the big

pay-off. I wonder where Cloud Nothing
slept last night, ripped

T-shirt, slurring something about caprice
and the neighbour's wife, tilted

vocabulary suiting the way his small red
hands slipped off

the patio railing. The wind kept
its pulse, blowing years

off our sunburnt backs, making our noise-
less conversations harder to hear

as we rode along in the back of a black
pick-up truck, coming home

to another king Autumn.

# Dirtbag

Simplicity is wonderful, a chance to forget
the watch, he thought, his thoughts tickled

by a burnt orange sunset. The earth sleeps in the curved
bed of his fingernails. He's dozing off in the hollow

of a mud speckled red truck, no longer red, next
to a mountain silhouette and the ghosts of bearded men

puffing up their chests in the onslaught of shadows.
The sky is at that moment between day and night.

Everything is still except the flames, defiant dragons
attacking the darkness, breathing in the cusp of twilight.

His trophies are memoirs, sealed with high fives
from like-minded friends. His kindred spirits

prefer to breathe on the edge of the earth, wide-eyed
and brimming in the shimmer of morning.

His wild inner pulse inks over the canvas, fearless
in the long gentle whisper of rivers that wander.

He is a lifestyle, a celebrity for evergreen trees.
And tonight, beneath one thousand American sunsets

in the desert lushness of sage and creosote, he is tangled
with dreams of tomorrow, his hair like a sandy beach.

He is mostly a picture, a fading serenade to the sky
being swallowed in Utah, being swallowed outside.

# NSFW

This is a story of mouthwash and double-jointed coitus.
It's all carpet, lip gloss and the crevasse of your blue jeans.

I'm frantic to park this white car in the shadows,
eager to massage the blouse off your shoulders, early

before the cold feet come cock blocking through the vents
of the dashboard, pulling your ass into a world of what-if's

and long after school specials on resisting feral instincts.
I once had sex in a blue Porta Potty. It was how you imagine.

Popping Viagra on the Ferris wheel, your tongue like cotton
candy, the carnie whipping us around faster and winking

wildly, his belt buckle a galloping black steed in heat.
Let's eat these snacks and go back to being naked acrobats.

I'm rising to the occasion, ready to be your treadmill,
perform these circus tricks mastered by the cocaine stars.

It's like making music the way we flicker bareback
beneath the full moon, panting, our pulse pushing past

it's resting rhythm, unfettered. That's the doorbell.
Invite Pizza Joe in, ask him to dislodge me from the rafters.

Here, wear this fake nose-moustache disguise while I take
the clinic through the hardest lesson. I know what this looks like.

I'm up to my elbows in K-Y Jelly and you keep calling me
the astronaut. The neighbours are parting their lips,

smelling the dirty laundry and posting pictures of what must
look like The Worm from over there. I'm disheveled,

our seams slowly unravelled, your thighs like magnets,
my disco balls all aglitter. Let's wash, rinse and repeat, again,

make the most of these wet dreams, but, Baby, who
the hell is Humpy Dangle? I've bounced back, groping

for a reason to care as our faces melt in this candlelit
sweatshop. Let's eat more pomegranates, whisper

our wishlists into cupid's canon, the squeeze play
in full orbit, our tongues raw and full of midnight hustle,

ready to burst the speech bubbles building off our grins,
mine — something about bushwhacking and the washing machine,

and yours — well, your dripping mouth formed the letter
O in a big, buoyant font, over and over and over and over.

# The Wide Mouth of Real Estate

This real estate agent drooled, eyes like stuffed money pits, voice like a bulldozer. This real estate agent thinks the market is made of swine and the view from over here is breathtaking. This real estate agent does back flips in the dirt, could sell an old shirt off her arched back. This real estate agent is in love with another real estate agent, dreams of owning a real honeymoon. This real estate agent has ideas, thinks we should get creative. This real estate agent thinks we're poised for an offer, thinks we're going to buy this pink coffin. This real estate agent hopes he isn't right. This real estate agent smells like old spice, looks like a burnt candle. This real estate agent blinks a lot, forgets to shake my hand. This real estate agent wants to be my lover, wants to seduce me with hot listings in Inglewood. This real estate agent is restless. This real estate agent is not trying to pressure us. He's just restless. This real estate agent wants us to be aware of an opportunity. This real estate agent puts it this way: Imagine you're driving home from work tomorrow, the sun is shining and feels warm on your face. Your favourite song is playing on the radio. Life is good. Now, imagine I call you on this drive and tell you this house, *your* house is sold. How would you feel? How deep would you sink? I imagine, here, that I actually own a cell phone. I imagine a weathered iron anchor sliding down my throat, weighting me, stomach like the bottom. It is here I envision myself on the shore of a small island, alone, content, surrounded by nothing; no movement, no question mark, no curse, no bad ties.

# Dead Raccoon

I am sitting in the courtyard of our house in Bankview,
jagged flagstones puzzled together like a child's toy.

A warm cup of Grizzly Claw on the table. *The Paris Review* open.
I'm peeling back the flesh of my poet head, trying to knuckle

down on a yellow canoe and Billy Collins at the bow.
His pencil out of breath, quiet at home. My focus slips

to the brown ants, moving in all directions like this round
table was a shopping mall. I espy the sparrow sketch

against the red bricks, painted by an old roommate who fell
steeply into the basement, shattering a five gallon glass jar

with his knee. His blood filled the cracks and chipped cement,
then crawled slowly beneath the washing machine.

A dusty *Pink Moon* plays through the window of the house
where my pregnant girlfriend cleans, cleans, and cleans.

Nick Drake sings, convincingly, of being younger than before,
but weaker and somehow the lilac trees agree, twisted trunks,

purple flowers gone with spring. I've just returned from N.B.
and I'm trying to read this John Poch poem now, but all I can think about,

suddenly, is driving to Hampton just yesterday with my father
and moving past a matted raccoon, an open heap in the rhubarb.

Of all the things I've seen on the highway, I am most like you.

# September Eleventh Zygote

Son, this isn't about airplanes, although
there is an adult version of vertigo, somewhere.

You arrive under a parliament of fluorescent
hospital lights. Hello, Little Little. Welcome.

You look iridescent on digital camera, your hurt
head looks like a purple yarmulke from the doctor

heaving on a rubber plunger with alarming force.
They invite me to sever the umbilical, Wharton's

jelly, all soft pasta blue, the sound of white sneakers
squeaking, but I watch you, listen for your first breath.

Son, you can't roam the galaxy with only one testicle.
I wonder about the design of your first sentence.

I am a rookie, moving through this new tunnel
with small intuitive steps, searching for the features

of my face in your smaller face. I am in love
with making you laugh, watching you bounce around

the crib, untainted smile five teeth strong, sunshine
for the plastic clouds I taped to your painted grey wall.

One day we will climb old geology, lift a glass
of single malt, live life like we are already dead.

Until then, let us finish this hair-raising allegory
of the alive, pale green pants with nobody inside

and, Nolan, when you breathe in the sky and swallow
the moon, how does it make you feel otherwise?

# Horoscopes

"My horoscope today was fifteen hundred pages long and in
annotated form it read: Bang you're dead." – ADAM DRUCKER

**Aquarius** (Jan. 20 – Feb. 18)
Even though life is a deserted candy shop,
you still relish the golden nectar of honey.
It's smeared all over your cracked lips.
All you have to do, this time, is lick them.

**Pisces** (Feb 19 – March 20)
The moon is aligned with your missteps.
Could be worse, bastard. Orthopedics?
Nah. I see a permanent slouch, plaid
shorts unbuttoned and a jack in the box.

**Aries** (March 21 – April 19)
The bird's nest is empty. On Tuesday
you will chant death to everyone but us
and watch the disparate flock vanish.
The bird shit on your viewfinder is new.

**Taurus** (April 20 – May 20)
Success is skin deep, you poet you.
You can find the treasured metaphor
of master craft in a slow oil leak or
the vicious snarl of your big brother.

**Gemini** (May 21 – June 20)
You've never paid for free cable.
You've named your grey cat Rimbaud.
You're convinced today is your day,
Even though that's painfully not true.

**Cancer** (June 21 – July 22)
If your roommate is a noise virtuoso,
saving bohemian women with lust
and you feel like a fading photograph,
sell the pawnshop, save the semblance.

**Leo** (July 23 – Aug. 22)
Need a segway or simple life support?
Burning bridges was a bad idea.
Don't fret. Take this for what it's worth:
You share a birthday with Obama.

**Virgo** (Aug. 23 – Sept. 22)
Libra is on cloud nine, lamenting
the loss of his romantic self.
You want to analyze horseshoes,
loosen probability in the tree house.

**Libra** (Sept. 23 – Oct. 22)
Today you are the antihero, willing
to leap from an airplane, tongue velvet,
the seal of your wit blown wide open.
The visions will only get more intense.

**Scorpio** (Oct. 23 – Nov 21)
This month is like a James Ellroy novel,
hardboiled and relentlessly pessimistic.
You'll make love to a melodramatic cross-
dressing jazz musician and die in the end.

**Sagittarius** (Nov. 22 – Dec. 21)
You're a lonely, drunk vessel between two
places you've never been. Take off
the beer goggles. You're a mermaid and
swimming has never been this fun.

**Capricorn** (Dec. 22 – Jan 19)
It is clearly unclear what it is like
to be you, here, at your sixth birthday,
bobbing for apples. Velvet Underground
on record. This year is an Indian summer.

# When the Neo-Nazis Came for Dinner

Now

I was fourteen and God,
reading books on perception

finding lost souls in the neighbourhood
while Dead Kennedys plucked my brother

and his drunk ghettoblaster.
I wore my suburban haircut with a yawn.

Earlier

in the rain, gliding
my skateboard like a rag doll

through waves of blank faces
and the blur of a busy street,

I was jostled by a skinhead
with eyes like a junkyard,

shovelled in the path of a long
rusty Buick blind in one eye.

He flapped weathered leaflets
on the freedom of speech and

with a swollen face, hate sang
off his lips in the cold rain.

Later

when the Neo-Nazis came for dinner

I served them sad puppets
stuffed with dead light bulbs

and for dessert,
we burnt the books they loved

and scraped their swastikas
onto the broken dinner plates.

# Kensington

All my friends do drugs,
        vitriolic and handsome,
        born with no ears.

They glow with early morning aura,
        roasted coffee and sunrays,
        bent and frozen in freeform.

They wax poetic on the corner,
        ungentrified lofts, good locations,
        sour grapes on the dresser.

Their swollen heads, unlike totems,
        stretching into cupboards
        craving cheap whisky and bread.

Tastefully undone, they wear shadows
        beneath electric lights, polishing
        sardonic bites beneath the moon.

Half-beards and cigarettes, stuffed
        ashtrays like graveyards, burnt
        with velvet imprints of soft seduction.

Their music is a gentle distorted buzz, only
        dim, drapeless living room.
        TV on channel blue.

They wear fading turquoise T-shirts:
        Feminist Chicks Dig Me.
        Existential Art Renegades.

They run with lush quotes, dead editorials,
    quitting time, ambitious goals;
    become immortal, then die.

# Druggy Pizza

The fringes of my face
were long, longer than five

o'clock. The wheels slanted,
limped into Winnipeg,

still waterlogged and Mitch
was swamped with plenty

of odd jobs. His sister spoke
to all sorts of people

near the pavilion but was frying
some other fish that day.

I needed more coffee and a hard
ticket but first one thing

and then another moving
sidewalk, past silent misfits.

Over Thunder Bay I breezed
with some lady who was not

young. Her teeth were stained
a rusty yellow and I pointed

to her beer and said was that
complimentary? She lowered

her guard and heavy coughed
through tales, splintered

in bad weather. In Toronto,
on the plane, I put my green

bag in the top compartment
next to a bouquet of bright

flowers and the brusque
stewardess, flustered mouth,

ushered me off the plane
having peddled my seat,

9A, to somebody else.
I crashed on my brother

Robb's couch and he cooked
Mediterranean sausage

at around six in the morning.
I was wearing my white Parquet

Courts T-shirt, the lucky one
with Lightnin' Hopkins framed

on the front. You ain't gon'
live always scribbled

beneath his crude sketch.
A little frayed, blotting words

in Montreal, when I quick
questioned a shy barista where

the 747 was and she spoke softly,
asked me if there was some-

place I was supposed to be.
On the bus, I slumped easy,

next to a blond dopey hipster
in a bowtie and S T A Y  G O L D

tattooed across his plump
knuckles. Auspiciously timed,

Luke buzzed up to Laurier
Metro with a grey beard

he said just exploded
haphazardly across his face.

I told him he looked old
but I was haggard, hauling

around this green duffel bag.
We made sandwiches, moseyed

through the plateau, drinking
cappuccino from Café Olimpico.

I took pictures of a Miles Davis
mural and Luke snapped his

fingers at a Shih Tzu, his film
casting an orbit on fossilled

faces of mostly men
ambling these sunny streets.

Alex cameoed into his window
later and I was vapid on tying

the knot tighter while Luke
laughed in disbelief, thought

another year was a little harsh,
I think. We double backed

towards the laundromat
passing a drab bank we once

slept in; it was hello winter
and Canada cold and Luke

lost the door key to his tiny
apartment in the backseat

of a taxicab. We drank 50 tall
beers at a dive bar with a sad

jukebox while his dirty laundry
swirled next door and I kept

thinking the rain was going
to come but it never really did

until maybe later, while we
were sleeping. The next day,

at Osheaga, Shane and I
took drugs, little pink pills

and I said he looked like
porno the way his deltoids

were sweating in the sun,
the naked heat teaching us

a thing or two. We were still
floating across the music

pushing from the speakers,
a thousand hands waved back

and forth and I felt certain
there was a home invasion

happening somewhere behind
my eyes, in the damp basement

of my *joie de vivre*. The first words
I spoke the next morning

was something like Jesus but
I really wonder what Karine

said because she thought
she was frozen. Not cold but

stuck, unable to bounce
from the grass slope she was

sort of praying on, where I left her
and Shane to boomerang

around the sea of sunbathing
animals, looking for an antidote

or maybe just some druggy
pizza but I didn't find

either. I disappeared with some-
thing organic and edible instead

while two pretty, but pregnant,
strangers whispered isn't this

fun in a way that seemed
clandestine to me. A beautiful

surprise the other said, nodding
with no apparent destination

in mind.

# The Regulars

Some men are made of cardboard, shrewd
      cut-outs from dull scissors.
Some men seal themselves in white envelopes,
      hope to be opened at a funeral.
Some men can talk about food, licking
      their fingers like desert spoons.
Some men bring home the groceries
      but forget to cut the mustard.
Some men treat love like half-assed art projects.

Some men use drugs as an animal club.
      Some have nicknames like Pill Wonder.
Some men can't play the harmonica,
      tie starry-eyed ambition with guitar strings.
Some men own the ocean with enough coin
      leftover to mortgage the vast sky.
Some men can't pay their bar tab, forget
      curb swerving on an old brown bicycle.
Some men draw a detailed maze by hand, hang
      obscure art by I-think-I've-heard-of-him.
Some men like spontaneous picnics and Thai soup.

Some men smell like poker chips and grave-
      yards, hold hot dice in warm light.
Some men like bags, putting them in rivers,
      then go pissing in the gold sand.
Some men shoot long guns like amateurs.
      They put dead mammals in wood frames.
Some men look good in hats, borrowed car keys
      and a red wine moustache.
Some men look better in wide sinister grins
      than some other men.
Some men dream of fat ATM machines.

Some men think cars sound lonely in the rain,
     and maybe worse at midnight.
Some men leap off towers, eat kryptonite
     and stock options. They can't bluff.
Some men waste words to dance dumbly
     with women in tight leopard skirts.
Some men spend their whole lives
     . looking for an ashtray.
Some men don't want to answer the phone
     because they know there are wild horses
     on the other side.

# Tilt Shift

"Sometimes when I close my eyes I hear a billion workers
in my skull, hammering nails from which all the things I see
get hung." – MATTHEW ZAPRUDER

I'm at the gallery, opening night; I've come
for the crab puffs. I'm gazing vaguely

at this stark daguerreotype of someone
being weathered in a tightly riddled cabin,

time drawn on his face like an honest workshop.
I'm aware that tonight is kind of rudderless,

a fine night to swim in the deep end, spill red
wine across secrets, laughing awkwardly

over omelets in the hazy imprint of morning.
This painting is subdued and quietly coloured,

nothing much to say with its cool vista blue.
An echo builds within the cracked chestnut frame.

A puzzled crowd gathers and on second thought
it jolts like a sapid construction site. Indeed,

the Esker is all abuzz now and this sprawling
capsule is shapeshifting, ejecting me in odd

directions, blurring my thoughts on death
and taxes. Wow! There! Beneath the arch,

majestic creature in pro curves! I'm lost
in the thump of some ghost orchestra rising.

I should be brazen, untie my tongue, impress
with quips on her magnetic appeal. Instead I sh-sh-

shuffle behind poorly punched clay. *Endorphins*
looks damaged like an exploding lantern,

an oblique kiss of light, a fractured still life,
scores of drunk fireflies. The hairs on the back

of my neck are like the legs of chairs.
Here we go, the bruised critic's darling,

the one I came to be seen seeing, pensive texture
wrapped around my face. Hmm ... it's full of blind

muscle, flesh that radiates, a brightly tortured map
to the pseudo-virgins, handmade by blushing velvet

pixies. Hello, Ruby, I think as she saunters off
in one wrong direction, flowing spontaneous towards

something mistakenly uncanny, propped up out
of context like a limited edition, gracefully clamped

to a crystal wine glass. Three bookish types step
back, make room for cynicism, darkly sneer

at the narrative; two boys, morals under attack,
kicking a tattered cat, a gateway act to arson or

an STI. Nuns grin, chug malt liquor near the trash.
In another dream, I'm floating in the margin,

wounded but making sense of the hazards. A bag
of nails, colourful snapshots and rough notes for future

romance. It starts with finding the words, but first
the ground, and ends with being tangled up

in a moment not long ago.

# Date Night

They lean in with open hearts,
moving in slow motion

in the Midwest. Man is out
to peel off her pants. Woman

wants Man to wear a bathrobe,
Neither knows of the other's

starts to dance. Man awkwardly
happy birthday to you, Woman.

glances into the frame, then
notice the audience, just an equinox.

hopping around the old TV set.
sharpens his pencil, sketches

her his genitals, but now she
into a cache that will be used

on the mystery of emotions
Man and Woman resurface handi-

yard into the grand attention
of something keenly nostalgic,

eyelids twitching, the narrative
towards an ordinary apartment

of sorts, wants Woman
fiddles with buttons on the camera,

play dead and pretend to be a natural.
hidden light bulb, until Woman

shuffles through the afternoon, sings
Woman trades knowing, coy

her eyes brush the window, doesn't
She is thrilled with the fish-out-of-water

Man runs fingers through hair,
Woman on all fours, really wants to show

is welling up, her tears splashing
in an upcoming warehouse exhibit

called Cracking the Hex, assuming
capped, ready to pivot out of the back-

span as someone on the precipice
something that sails out of dreams.

# Shudder Island

A friend once said that Vargas Island
was haunted and I half held

> my breath as we pummelled
> each ridge, moving north

through the disquietly named
Deadman Islets. The waves

> swelled, bashed the boat assiduously
> and things felt vaguely

cinematic the way my son's eyes slung
shot from awe to uncertainty

> in a slow, crooked time-lapse.
> Everything was grey; the dead

sky, the ocean, the vessel
as it swirled around sharply,

> chasing some blind enormity
> barely lifting out of the bay.

Strange barnacles billowed across
the white froth and Nolan said

> he saw something but I'm not sure
> he really saw anything the way

the boat rose and twisted
steeply between the haystacks.

The sky was shaking, beautifully
dim as the mountains towered

ominously and all together
the beast seemed thoroughly

inebriated. Darragh squealed,
pointed out the big picture

as a harbour porpoise dipped in
and out and into the water

but in all honesty we didn't know
that at the time. Nolan, more

pale, searched quizzically, blurted
something about the terrifying

depth and we all agreed
but maybe didn't say it aloud,

just cool pulsating to the Captain's
tales as the boat drifted wild.

Village slaughters, ingenious
cliff dwellers, living tightly

in Mexico in a small leaky tent
with his girlfriend and a ransom

of dreaming pups nesting
their tanned, desultory heads

while sunken wolves with thinner
ribcages howled and paced

faceless, untethered beneath the moon.
Unsettling, he said and now

Nolan, clearly perturbed,
wondered out loud if I was really

　　　　fearless, willing to strong-arm
　　　　the concurrent violence

churning madly under the boat
if he were, you know, washed out

　　　　by accident. I felt nauseous.
　　　　It was so hot in the cabin

but the Captain seemed reluctant
to open the window. In fact,

　　　　he seemed a little rudderless,
　　　　pausing then jarring heads softly

into a shudder with an anecdote
on Hamlet, a beleaguered sea otter,

　　　　slapjacking a colony of seals,
　　　　an incredulous urge, no doubt,

to commit the most lurid acts
on a bewildered baby seal.

　　　　Tourists with invisible eyes
　　　　mistook this affliction for affection

until Hamlet, tired of speaking
his frank language of love

bit the head clean off and waved
it around like a Shakespearean

celebrity. The boat scudded
gaining a kind of frazzled

momentum, Nolan cajoling
for my answer. I gulped, my face

tumbling closer to the most
meaningful silence I could muster,

a quiet that would become more clear,
with patience, in the course of time.

# Short Story

We placed the empty bottles on the open window sill. Your insults were like glass and outside the leaves were an electric yellow. We smoked cigarettes in the streets, rode old bicycles through this dreamcity. Our music was loud, drifting off the boulevard. I read you punch drunk poems of bad lovers under a tumultuous sky and together we felt like something was finally unravelling. Later, we traipsed into the afterhours, staggering. I was secretly in love with the way you slept in the tall grass, your face masked in a warm sunset. You kiss like a sledgehammer. I am like dead meat or heavy traffic and we are a short story.

# Mirror

Today I imagined a solemn man
      with a surly beard, a nutty barnacle
that dawdled half a decade.

I imagine this wire stone untrimmed,
      discoloured in rich nicotine.
I imagine him wearing green plaid shirts

ripped at the elbow, collar
      kind but ruffled, blue jeans
no longer blue. I think he is chopping

birch today, near the cedar cabin,
      sun peaking through leafy still trees,
man's best friend beige and indolent,

pleased with juddering squirrels in the morning.
      He is fixing the chainsaw now. Yes,
playing it like a musical instrument,

felling timber near the cracked red canoe.
      His fingers are buttered with oil, trenched
with grease, breath smothered in moonshine.

      He lives alone these days.

Later, I imagine him slashing his woolly beard,
      his rough face a corridor of the past.
It's cathartic — unbinding this heavy mask, concealing

the belly of the bathroom sink.
      Later, driving in a chasm, a void
without context, he is recognized by no one,

not even someone        not even
      a lonely muddleheaded man in town
he once called a friend.

# Beyond the Windmills

I can't even see your face. I hate sleeping
alone. In the haze of stronger aphrodisiacs,

I try to speak without saying anything.
Brush your hand. I want to French kiss.

Beneath the windmills. When a man loves
a woman he drowns. He can't think of some-

thing charming to say, can't even hear your
breath. The wind lashing its invisible roar,

sweeping away thoughts of tussled hair,
fingers burrowed, your denim skirt parked

around imprisoned hips. I want to be burned.
I'll be Mr. Good with grass stains woven

on my skin. Make movies in the crow's nest.
But we are still, sidelong to the rotor blades

swooping down lonely in the night sky.
And my unbeknownst sweetheart sneezes,

snaps the near silence with a vapid mist,
your legs like glued scissors. My heart in orbit,

hurries to the end when you flip on your hips,
your breasts like headlights, your eyes born to lie.

You lean closer, gently whisper into my ear,
I think you said you were falling in love

       with clean energy.

# Along a Dark, Wet Street

I have never passed this close to death,
rubbernecking on the narrow highway,

gawking at some commotion in the ditch.
I see tall supercops batting their eyelashes

in the Autumn downpour. They nod and
crunch shattered windshields, their yellow

raincoats bright in the steamy headlights
of a crumpled palindrome, a caved racecar.

The scream of the engine is loud; I can see it,
the accident unfolding on the wet street.

I can see the colours of the crash, red pastels
smudged from the rain, her face like a shattered

flowerpot. And the boy, missing a hand, looks
like a fire pit in the backyard of a nightmare.

I can see myself reaching across the cockpit
for a quick nip from a flask of dry whisky,

car drifting across the faded yellow. I can see it,
the steel jaws of life peeling apart an engine,

my engine in the heat of a summer twilight.
I can see my disfigured face, bloody and split

in the rearview mirror, I can almost hear
a dog bark arbitrarily in the distance.

# How to Make Movies

It's hard to say when exactly my father's
advice flushed through the backyard, ether

passed around the campfire, mangled
anatomy poking wood pallets doused in gasoline.

Thinner blood makes me solipsistic, self-
loathing, aching for the warm rabbit hole.

My girlfriend was a bomb shelter. Then she split.
Hubris, she said. The stars were out that night

but I couldn't swallow. I hate the math of epitaphs.
After seeing a man's face clipped off by a lawnmower

the word trust comes with a sense of electricity.
I bought the fly swatter between hills of trepidation.

I keep it wrapped in a wad of lazy hospital slings.
I'd stumble into violence but there's nothing happening

here. My best friend is not lucid, hyped up on mind
benders, craves a test drive under the street lights, calls

it the upper hand glimmer. I'm cracked, swivel towards
the window, rewinding the last moments, knuckles

a fantastic white, murky blood still in the toilet. Tonight
I return the favour, spit out the battered motive.

This is for him, his Band-Aid philosophy, his rotten
antenna; when you're just short of potential, life is soggy,

he'd say, a tough hump through the trenches. It's a long
clip of monotonous b-roll and goddamn it! Could I pay

attention for two seconds? Time is being swallowed and
what the hell will I say for myself when the credits roll?

# 17 Girls

The first belly bloated into a silent squeal,
an echo of wild flowers rose near the pink bleachers.

      The second became unglued, sidled up
      to the frozen faces in the cafeteria with a half-smile.

Number three beat the odds, unconditionally lost,
spoke as if the day's pop song was a long range forecast.

      Seconds since insemination and number four
      shelled out for a year's worth of metallic Similac.

The fifth teen inked a sappy love letter to Ellen Page
about crossing t's and dotting i's, but she misspelled intercourse.

      The optics on number six resembled a worm deep
in a red apple, her faded pink underwear getting a little tight.

I just want to be loved, said number seven, helping
an askew homeless man shop for leather belts.

      Here's a toast to number eight, homerun Sally
      with her blue demeanor and nothing much else to do.

Next was number ten, who shaved the beard off the boy
who was known to make omelets for number nine.

      Number eleven was all pathos, lips like training wheels,
      hips like flags lifting into the night her parents went out.

Seems to be something amiss in the bottom drawer of number
twelve's dresser, namely her prized Playboy stopwatch.

Unlucky number thirteen was a bit like a banged up
Plymouth, naughty hair, skin deer hoof tough.

The pact was a no-brainer for fourteen, so friendless for long
nights. Sex on the Beach and ironic catcalls is just the thing!

Number fifteen dressed in a large green parachute,
snorted Adderall and unlatched her knee brace.

400 menstruations, number sixteen approximated.
Minus 9 as she blew out the scented birthday candles.

Pretty seventeen pushed and pushed and pushed
and the entire motley crew of rain men picked up

their hard to believe tales of smashed windshields
and went screaming for the locks they tied to their lips.

# Nitpicking and Cantankerous Quarrelling

You're unromantic.
I feel alive when I'm alone.
Why do you fold pages, split the spine?
Hush before I break a wine glass.
Pretend to be a gentleman.
Adolescent.
Spell divorce.
You're so blind and all brightly vacant.
Trim your eyebrows. TV roadblocks.
Remember when you got fired?
Thanks for the dead daisies, Dick.
I love you, November.

You're like a revolver.
Let's do the waltz of the lonely motel.
Why do you trash talk, face a dented anvil?
I need a zealous blonde, a spelunker.
Innocence, a liar's walking stick.
Mannequin.
O-n-e-s-t-e-p-a-h-e-a-d.
And this soup has large onions.
Is *The Saddest Music in the World* on?
For necking with the secretary?
My pleasure, wizened hag.
You're the parts, I'm the labour.

# The Pigeons Flock in Awe

around the dozing statue, zzzzz
wide amongst open wings.

The long curtains, paralyzed,
twisting off worst thoughts,

head swelling in odd angles.
We keep one foot in a bronze

bucket. It takes many clocks
to build a proper pawnshop,

double bed in the back, dead
celebrities clipped and tacked

to the post. The prize today
is inadequate, a strangled half-

heart. But there goes the lifetime
collective, boarding the carousel

in some Eros frenzy, fainting
like patients out from the shadows,

this morning too by email.
We need fifty wizened hands

lampin' on this perch, perception
amiable, gold package edible.

It's borderless being born again
and then born again, bundled

as caricature with a pesky
erection and a black torn ego

topped full with a toothy
ambivalence poised to stale.

Tonight we sleep or celebrate.
Tomorrow, we begrudgingly

feed these stout-bodied birds
a taste of the new enormity,

carefully open the handcrafted
corridor and wait for the utterly

speechless. But of course
things are never that simple.

# Scavenger Hunt

A rather large unruly group of critics
pace outside of my house, wielding

light bulbs. Red inquisitions dangle
off their tongues like pitchforks.

They yelp about brain tissue, waving
placards made with broken pencils.

They've kidnapped my muse, threaten
to silence her forever with verbose edicts

on academia's great hunger, a kill list
swelling in their ribcage undercurrents.

They want to know how I write poems,
intend on clawing back my scalp

with kitchen knives and a device that opens
sealed envelopes. What do they think

they'll find? A tattered script of instructions?
An abstract logo speckled with imagination

goo? Are they thirsty for confession typed
onto the bare cortex spelling out some magic

potion of the creative mind, kind of sticky
but illuminating nonetheless, especially

when brewed with a borderless uneven eye?
I try to ignore them but the panic and squealing

is unbearable, chanting dreadful things
in bright marathon colours. They go on and on

and on, one voice after another, chasing
a naked score, a futile desire to harness

the untamable, the echo in tone monotonous.
It's getting louder and then a butterfly

lifts off nearby, zigzagging wildly through
the open air until landing on a dimpled

grey rock about the size of a wrestler's fist.
Two people wander into the wilderness

either bored or wanting to taste somebody
more prolific. Another grabs the grey stone

and hurtles it through a window of my house,
smashing my temple, knocking me dark,

breaking my chain to reverie. When I awake
they are surrounding, eyes like fireworks.

I can smell butter frying in the kitchen.
My hair is on fire, fingernails pulled from

the comfort zone, my tongue flat, spiked
between books on Anatomy and Poetry

for Dummies, respectively. My train
of thought is derailed as they poke around

the left frontal lobe, peeling back pink folds,
determined to fiercely mine this mind.

It is with much effort I am able to slowly
mouth this cold, weightless clue

on the direction of their curious scavenger
hunt: You are looking in the wrong spot.

# Holding Out

There is a league of men
on the toilet, quietly

improving maxims, taking
the ol' oyster mantra

for a deep tissue massage.
I'm hiding, really tumbling

beneath some shotgun
house, my eyeballs dead-

bolted behind a quasi-diet
of dead animal parts.

All the good detectives
keep evaporating, grand-

fathered into the cotton
candy coloured clouds,

barely a dispirited hunch
coursing between them.

I hate to say it but
I'm a little miffed at being

stuck in this maze of village
idiots, elected to wave

their wife's vibrators around
like some desperate plea

bargain. All the good ideas
just kind of sit there benignly

in a flyblown box, perched
on a mountain of saggy

user survey cards. Seems simple
enough but the strangers

are starting to balk at those
things they were told

were beautiful. They're
acting like animals, actually,

throwing toilet paper over
the rooftops, lying bare-

back out on the bike paths,
waiving the right to be word-

less around bigwigs. Parasites
snack in black taxicabs near

the park. Listen, can you
really trust a man with a Band-

Aid across the sunburnt
bridge of his soul?

# Blemish

The fridge flopped on the front lawn,
       dead thud, the door flapping open

briefly like an expired exhale. Butchered
       meals pitched around, painting

aimless in the cool coffin; cottage cheese,
       tuna salad, a carton of brown eggs.

Behind us, inside the house, walled memories
       scuttled by fists of cheeseburgers, gangster

rap maimed, bloodsucking through a broken window.
       Dints of drunken Sharpie tags, misogynist

slanguage littered the hallway to the bathroom
       like some antsy ghetto soapbox,

a tepid distraction amidst the rummaging up-tempo.
       The phone lines had been halved,

furniture trampled in odd places like the charcoal
       couch perched on the roof.

The television burst, an exploding face transplant,
       jagged glass jarring the dark space

revealing a brain maze of wire. The life of the party
       looked shatterproof, some dude with green

eyebrows shotgunning cans of Moosehead
       in the kitchen, abandoned shirt, telling muddy

jokes to a squad of pretty stoned degenerates
lamping on broken beer bottles.

The house was being hollowed, things
zipping around me like a skateboarder

somersaulting into a missing sister's bedroom
wall with something I might have mistook

for vehemence. The emasculated host formed
different opinions with a black eye near midnight,

his girlfriend screaming at some asshole holding
the microwave. Out back, swaying on the patio,

tattooed hippies junk starred with sticky chronic,
blunts thicker than index fingers, frayed

voices leaping over Phish in Montreal, so warped
on six tabs of sunshine acid.

I felt so bad for the kid's parents but didn't
have the resolve to stop this nirvana,

just kept looking for the wild raccoon
I saw slink deeper into the backyard

of American elm and Red Oak trees. Sirens
leaned into the wind adding some cold

fiction in the distance, or at least that's how it felt
standing in the middle of bored vandals,

swirling around to *Dookie*, vomit drying on my T-shirt
    and my friend's sneakers which she slipped

off her feet sweetly, walking home not once
    looking back through the bypass except sometimes

I think about what happened next when his parents
    pulled into the driveway, vacation ease

cracked widely, chewing on the aftermath. They
    must've been half-boiled, drowning in fear and

fury, or at the very least felt slightly blemished, no longer
    credulous to the innocence of youth,

to the unfinished business dimmed-out on the roof.

# Beneath All Great Centre of Things

is a hummingbird, a lurking *ping*
that ricochets off the tin interior.

We stumble forward, never cartooned,
painted with blue eyes as the grand gesture

below bellows up, guttural voice, grey veins,
ominous vice. A cracked violin persists,

evocative hue beyond the murmur of women
giving birth, pregnant with bilious poets, glib

with blank cheques in five second thunderstorms.
Men toasting cold beer in the bottomless eye.

Lucky women giving birth to machines,
no candied hitchhikers stuck to their socks.

Beneath all breathing centres boys swim
with barbarians, looking for the centre

of the centre of the holler dollarproud,
unwrapping dry roses on marble tabletops,

kissing puff pieces of the bad-humoured.
Bald juries sing the rust and ache of the tin.

# My First Night in Paris, Eight Years Ago

There is an angry man mid-scream
friendless, tying knots

on the face of another man
with big doubled fists.

I listen to them scowl. The violent mess
dumping blood into their bucket eyes

while the lonely Paris wind
rattles the cracked window

of my dive in the 6th arrondissement.

I rise from my bed with a broken back
board and Sarah rolls over facing the moon.

I splash cold Paris water onto my face,
rub my blue eyes and piss in the bidet.

Out on the cobblestone, the men hug
and tumble, drag their red flesh towards a victory —

soaking blood into the moustache of one.

The other, dancing with murky shit-kickers
beneath an orange glow of a tall lamppost.

Welcome to Paris, Monsieur.

# What Men and Women Do Alone

is pantomime sharply
out of the bedroom.

> They host a homegrown
> gag reflex, politely.

They serrate the words
on the walking tour,

> flimsy smiles at neighbours.
> Men and women bottle

the unspoken bits
until the body shapes

> of terse nouns explode into
> a blizzard; a battleground

on repeat, daily
reminders — long lines

> at the love factory.
> They try to renovate

the reasons with ear-
plugs and blind spots,

> hand jobs in camouflage.
> Men and women blur

at the television, swap
the family for strange

        flesh, burning at midnight
        in a backseat, busy.

Busy calling back casual,
busy adjusting the drapes.

# Somethings, Revealed: Degenerating

I've always liked the idea of wearing two hats, you know, something
for the day job and then something else, more sinister,

for the sickness.        My disposition is, largely, unpredictable.

I'm like an illumination one minute, scurrying across a damp basement,
into the shadows, revealing cobwebs and curled boxes of forgotten things.

Blink.

I'm an infinite darkness, stuccoed with hang-ups, bleached hair, strange stories
for hands. You just never know how lucid I'll dream.

Also, I ran over the red tricycle.        Intentionally.

Basically,

I am Letterman on acid. I don't even remember the accident.

I'm vain, a real open curtain.

I really hate the alimony, but snipping throats of your tulips helps.
Suppressing things I'd regret.

Tonight, I'm pale faced, ghost-like near the sink,
thinking of the last goddamned thing you said to me before you left,

blood mucking your front teeth,

my dick like a wand in the window, you said, quite frankly, "You need help.
        Get some fucking help."

IV

# The Boy and the Bottomless Lake

This is a tale about a boy and his bottomless lake. The boy lived in a tattered wood cabin near a dense grove of cedars with his mother and her lonely midlife. Beneath somber skylines on the outskirts of marriage and divorce, she tortured herself in roughly textured relationships with bent men.

The boy sat quietly on the backburner, fixing the broken transistor radio, juggling knives and making long movies in his mind. Together, the boy and his remote mother paused on the shore of a deeper misunderstanding.

Often, the boy would meander alone through the cedar grove, running his soft fingers across the trunks of green giants, thinking of a new motion picture. He was in love with weaving strange, beautiful epics. The hours would blur and the sun would slice the day in half.

Sometimes, he would fall asleep beneath his favourite towering cedar for days, the one with arms like a tired grandfather. His head drifting in and out of another lucid dream reel, grand worlds he produced bound only by the depth of his imagination.

One day, the boy shot and killed his mother with a glance. He then crawled into the bathtub and drowned himself with tears. The market of his imagination swarmed through his body searching for an exit. Outside, above the whispering cedars, the moon littered the face of the bottomless lake with applause.

# Property Taxed

The suburbs are surrounded by black tire mountains.
A yawning riptide discolours the scorched landscape.

The addictive contents of OxyContin canisters litter
the red pipes of residents. A guitar, no strings, gutted

in the grass. The Institute of Urban Redevelopment reports
of locusts gnawing the black brains of hungry house pets.

The sirens are limp. Backyards are graves and totems
of propane tanks. Smart Cars look stupid overturned.

The white fence has splintered, peeled skin, grit lines
sprinkled with the blood of bad ideas. From an armoured

tour bus it looks artistic; a starving xylophone in war bones.
The gangsters still have meth haircuts, burning billboards

of high stake handshakes, recruiting baby piranhas fresh
off the boat, hell bent. Without pesticides, the lawns

are blowing, perfectly wild, albeit a little neglected with
graffiti spray cans and toxic DMT portals. A radio crackles

half jokes from a comedian about the reason birds stoop,
sing Nirvana melodies. Poodles are pit bulls, anxious to taste

the lazy tongues of toddlers in Odd Future T-shirts. Geriatrics
huddle in a wooden ship planted near a charred Walmart.

They refuse to leave. This is their home. Iris even smiles
but when she opens her mouth it's all gravel and nasty ash.

The art of Banksy seduces the tall barriers that separate
the life static; a growing gallery of hip stencils for the wives

of architects that zip along the bright inner city bike paths.
We are pedestrians down to bar fight, building bone marrow

for the big siesta, the bomb packed in the ass of black sheep
and shoved into the night beyond the glow of expensive

city lights. We are scared blood donors, eating full buckets
of blueberries for their wealth of antioxidants, ingesting

neo sex pop for dessert. I'm willing to further bend the arch.
We shop at urban format boutiques in search of bargains

on bullets and peach cobbler. We stand in the lofts breathing
quinoa everything, wearing hats made from recycled egg shells,

fingers curled around polished sets of commemorative spoons
on the great reverse, the day the hatch broke and our dream

of little utopia rose up pure and simple like there was always
an absence of gravity to begin with.

# Zombie National Park

The flesh hung off his face
like a ripped flag, moaning

at the sun, limping
with a rabid incoherence.

We sipped iced lattes safely
in the rusted car, busted

speakers twisted out some dry
talk radio about a whizzing

asteroid. They were near
in the distance, cognizant

of our human scent, macabre
and undead, their limbs

like the soft insides of vegetables.

The wardrobe was pure
murder, predictably tattered,

sleeves rolled high above
the humeri like a mad butcher.

This one is all garish necktie,
fishing in black hummus under

the strips of his ribcage.
And this one wears a pink

hepcat dress, stained apron,
cooking up some lopsided orgy.

My God! This view is incredible!
Precious post-apocalypse at dawn.

Hey kids, look! Baby zombies
leeching the body art off some poor

bastard, purple intestines swing,
insatiable appetites gorging

with a rotten overbite in this remark-
able darkness. Pass the park map.

Who's hungry?

We gun it for Decomposing
Arch, traversing lifeless silhouettes

in the dirt, immortalized against
our iPhone Instagram, apple red

arms outreached like an awkward
handshake. We stop to ponder

the curious solace of Riga Mortis
Ridge, an impressive landmark

that makes my eyes wobble.
The origins of the first scream,

but, frankly, it's hard to enjoy
with the graffiti spilling out

of sun burnt, bickering kids
in the backseat, and for a hot

second I consider running
past the roadside carcass

and the glut of eager tourists
gathered outside of their comfort

zone, debating the pandemic
and the toxins that threaten

the lost souls of the afterlife.
I've been here before, raising

eyebrows, this violent smell
of nostalgia pushing me over

the granite boulders, away
from the intrepid kids screaming

and pounding on the car windows.
Further now, across the bone

marrow littered in the depths
of this sanctioned deathtrap

until I arrive, unscathed,
high above the restless groans

that echo through the speckled
canyon walls of where the once

ebbing veins of the electric
and majestic Blood River flowed.

# House Key

The busted slur of family, the tree
as rotting plum. Hair — drab and thinning,

      a loveseat for sunburns. Dreams
      are overwhelmingly overcast, reruns,

feeble with incivility. My wife is meek,
wobbles uncontrollably in some dark attic.

      My son yelps to Death Grips, waltzing in a
      rap sheet of stolen iPhones. His ego billows

like circus tents. Virgin daughter, now pregnant,
peddles grass, hand gestures like Johnny Cash.

      A muted piece of the puzzle has dribbled
      beneath the stained sofa, but I feel lethargic.

Cotton eyes, numb spine, awesome headache.
I daydream of erasing the boss, shaving

      her moustache with razor blades, hot
      coffee in her weathered, stoic face.

Colleagues whisper, weave true lies, but
somehow dance in mirrors, sign the letterhead.

      I say absolutely nothing. It seems the branch
      snapped out of context, splintered the lifeline.

The convincing impression faded, an oblique
splatter under the dimmer glare of gurus.

      Those books are now closed, the storm
      growling, the front door left slightly ajar.

# The Cannibals of Sichuan

The bare limbs
     of once pleasant
peasants are outreached, closing

the wooden shutters
     on tarnished
men. A sweet, white mud

clogs their intestines,
     makes their bellies
bloat and scream.

Runzhi smiles,
     green-coated
gums, playing cards

with submissive
     women.
Smelted door knobs,

pots tossed into a furnace
     does little to quell
the twitching lips

of generally quiet kids.
     To daughters
of starving fathers — RUN!

Eighty percent
     of the village
wants to eat you.

Eponymous neighbours
            plot, patching
traps to capture the nameless

under seven, while mom
            prays for big game
from her slumping

veranda. Your bony brothers
            prance through
the house insatiably,

hoping you will taste
            as good
as your sister.

# Doomsday Parade

We have the honeybees, asleep
     in our steel suitcase. Everything

is burning, ghost trees are glowing,
     lighting up the melancholy

of wildlife advisers. An acerbic taste
     sits in our mouth, craving

the phantom juice of watermelon.
     The neonicotinoids, they said,

were not murky, not really breaking
     glass into the food chain.

This thing, this twisting was predictable.
     A brusque wave of backlash

beginning to swell, ego tripping
     down the dark well

of the collective mind, lawn signs intrepid
     with it's now or never man

scribbled like an exploded afterthought
     and awaiting further instructions.

We're eating real cashews built
     on the back of shards of plastic.

Young bees pound on the bacon
     and we rip off the tourniquets,

tailgating the sirens, screaming,
        drooping through the doomsday

parade, past loose pedestrians en route
        to the bio-dome, offshore

from mass confusion and this biting
        diaspora. It takes time to inoculate.

It takes time to adjust the sprinklers
        and clip the requests of home-

sick hotel guests clutching long nostalgic
        lists of their favourite foods,

recipes stuffed into their jeans.

# Emergency Exit

I pretend my wife is away
on business, empty

the drawers onto the floor.
Vision is a little gauzy,

thoughts dog-eared next
to loosely formed sentences.

I'm putting up flyers
with scattered tacks on the wall

of this unhinged guru,
winking morosely.

He says to stimulate the wind
that's missing. I'm passed out,

skinny on the hardwood floor,
dreaming of driving

to Bloomington. Honey?
Let's entertain the neighbours

tonight, as I drunk shuffle
through the laundry, derelict

grin, mounds of crud
in my black eye. Status

updates howl, all caps,
gnashing teeth at old friends.

Look, I'm harnessed and dizzy,
prefer to ping pong through

a triple crown, sick of this stubborn
stump. I can't sleep,

chew on the bad taste of regret
in just my stained pajama top.

I'm back in the kitchen
picking at scabs near the sink,

delicately tie this apron
across the lacerations,

do not completely register
the voices cocked back

near my temple,
cutting the power lines

and pushing me freely
into the air, unfettered

but with no place to run.

# The Return of Whoop Dee Do

You changed your mind, thought otherwise,
the eponymous jackpot useless on the bitter

inside of a doomed compromise. Where did you
leave your old new hat? The bucket list? The damn

wherewithal? This is it, your second chance, bastard-
no-longer, the conjecture tamed, the meddlers hushed.

Meanwhile roll those sleeves to a less reluctant level.
It'll take more than pallid groans and elbow grease

to get you out of this one. Transcend freely, Bud.
Stretch out ungainly and palm this dark thumb-

tacked patchwork for a fading map to the cake matrix.
Gobble gobble. You'll need it. The whole enchilada.

Leave behind the beaglepuss, the buoyant apparatus
and the echo of a transgressive ee cummings poem.

Quick question though, if you were to do it all over
would you do it in high fidelity with a faster download

speed? Me neither. Let's shimmy shimmy, earth people!
Stargaze from a large crate of plums, far, far away from

dark, tight corners and wizened, idle gravediggers.
Freely, into the inebriated air holding our funny bones

and a taste for something least of all distinguished.
I suppose this is the life you want to live, right? Sunlit

with no nostalgia, lost strangers with nothing left
to lose, breaking character ad nauseam because why

not? That's the *je ne se quoi* of the infinite shit storm,
the next soliloquy and why you keep running through the door.

## About the Author

John Creary has had his poetry widely
published in Canadian literary journals
including *The Best Canadian Poetry in
English 2011, Arc, Event, Grain, CV2,
Fiddlehead, Vallum, subTerrain,* and *The
Antigonish Review.* He was awarded the
Calgary Literary Kaleidoscope Under-
graduate Award for Creative Writing in
2008. *Escape from Wreck City* is his debut collection of poetry. He
currently lives in Calgary.